# CONTENTS

S0-AFB-270

# INTRODUCTION

I am very grateful to the publishers for giving me the opportunity to say in public what I have been thinking and talking about privately for years. Preparing this book has given me the chance to take a closer look at coaching and I have come to realize just how much I enjoy it. I have been a fully qualified coach for years, but during the "shoots" for the illustrations, I have to say that my enthusiasm got going again.

Soccer is a wonderful game and if I can add to it by coaching when I stop playing then I will be

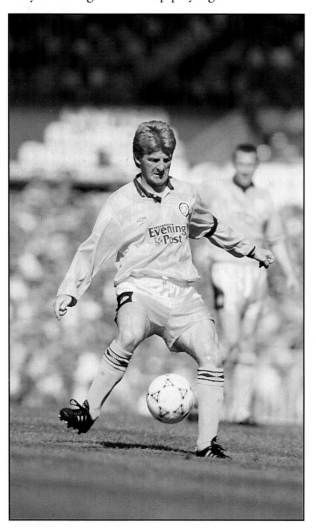

more than delighted to do as much as I can.

One of my biggest worries about coaching is allowing young players to reach their full potential. In a nutshell, I believe children play organized 11-a-side soccer too early. Basically, children under ten years old should not play the 11-a-side game. It would be far better for players this young to play 7-a-side soccer. This would allow them to play in all positions, on smaller fields, with smaller goals. Youngsters playing 11-a-side tend to be assigned to one position and to remain in that position. In my view, that is far too early for a youngster to be molded into a certain role. By being allowed to gain experience of different positions—which will happen in 7-a-side games—a youngster will develop more all-around skills which will be a benefit in whatever position is eventually chosen.

There is too much pressure on young athletes these days. When I was a kid I played for at least four hours a day without any strain. I found out by myself when it was time to pass the ball and when it was time to dribble it. When I was nine years old I did not need anyone to shout and scream at me. A call from a teammate or a kick on the shins from an opponent made me aware of when to get rid of the ball!

As a youngster I was allowed to think for myself but I find that, today, young children are not allowed to do that. Street soccer was a very popular pastime when I was young, but this is not so anymore and I would like to think that 7-a-side soccer could replace the street soccer we used to play. In my young days, naturally gifted players started in street soccer—not in a league for under-8s. No one taught me to play offside (thankfully at that age) or pressure the ball—I found it all out for myself.

I am not against youngsters being coached at an early age—but that should be done on an

# GETTING STARTED IN
# SOCCER

# GETTING STARTED IN
# SOCCER

## Gordon Strachan

 **Sterling Publishing Co., Inc.   New York**

### Acknowledgements

There are many people to thank for their help and co-operation in putting together this book. In particular I would like to thank my old friend and playing teammate, Mark McGhee, for allowing us to use Reading Football Club's excellent training facilities and, of course, the ground's owner Martin Deaner. Many thanks also to the boys of the Reading youth team (pictured below) who provided enthusiastic and skillful assistance throughout the photographic session. A particular thank you is due to Alfred Galustian whose youth coaching methods I have long admired. Alfred provided invaluable assistance with regard to the dribbling exercises and methods of beating a man. Thanks too to Graham Morgan of Adidas who provided the players' kits and indeed my own! Lastly many thanks to Don Warters, who helped me to put my ideas into words during the course of several enjoyable afternoons.

**Library of Congress Cataloging-in-Publication Data Available**

2 4 6 8 10 9 7 5 3 1

Published 1994 by Sterling Publishing Company, Inc.
387 Park Avenue South, New York, N.Y. 10016
Original edition published in 1993 in Great Britain by
Chancellor Press, an imprint of Reed Consumer Books Limited
under the title *Gordon Strachan's Step-by-Step Soccer Skills*
© 1994 by Reed International Books Limited
Distributed in Canada by Sterling Publishing
c/o Canadian Manda Group, P.O.Box 920, Station U
Toronto, Ontario, Canada M8Z 5P9

*Produced by Mandarin Offset*
*Printed and bound in Hong Kong*
*All rights reserved*
Sterling ISBN 0-8069-0834-3

individual level. Games are for enjoyment and self-expression. We can show the young how to develop individually and I hope that this book will help in that direction.

When I watch youngsters training I feel they do too much running. I see people making young kids do sit-ups and press-ups, which is nonsense because kids at that early age should not even think of doing push-ups. Their muscular development is limited at that stage and doing push-ups could result in their suffering a hernia, muscle strains and other ailments later on.

Coaches who look after young teams have told me that they do not have sufficient equipment. They say they have only three or four soccer balls and, in the same breath almost, ask me to go along to an awards ceremony to present 300 trophies—where did the money come from for those, I ask myself? Surely that money could be better used for equipment to help develop individual skills.

I suppose it is not surprising that coaches of

young teams and their young players like to win trophies. But I would say to such coaches that they would experience far more pleasure from seeing one of their players truly excel. You never know, the player might even go on to write a book saying that the guy who helped him most was his first coach!

Parents can be of help by not pushing their children too hard. I've seen parents who put an incredible amount of pressure on their children to win. But no matter how much shouting they do from the sidelines it will never make their kids better soccer players. I have sometimes seen 10-year-olds make rash tackles on other boys merely because their fathers have wound them up so much that they simply fly into the tackle.

Another thing that annoys me are those coaches who shout at kids during a game, telling them in a frenzied manner what they should have done. The best way to tell them is after the game—in a calm and civilized manner.

Most of the moves or skills we have tried to show in this book are ones you can practice with your friends and teammates, and you do not need to be under the supervision of anyone.

Having got all that off my chest, it only remains for me to say that I hope you enjoy the book. It has been great fun compiling it and I hope you will find that it helps you to become a better player.

*Gordon Strachan*

# WORLD CUP

# SOCCER RECORDS

**M**odern soccer has come a long way since the first rules were drafted in Cambridge University in 1848. It is now the world's leading team game. More countries are affiliated to FIFA than to the United Nations.

It is the sport of the people—even the poorest boys in the poorest countries can play, needing no more equipment than an improvised ball and a couple of sticks, rocks, chalkmarks or jackets for a goal. And every one of those boys can become as rich and famous as Pele or Maradona. At worst, they will have picked up enough feeling for the game to be able to appreciate the skills of future superstars as they watch them in the world's stadiums or on television.

The climax of the soccer calendar is the World Cup, the finals of which are held every four years in those even-numbered years which do not see a summer Olympic Games, the only rival to the World Cup as an international sporting bonanza.

When the United States of America won the right to host the 1994 World Cup finals, soccer took a step forward in the most powerful country in the world. Yes, I know the U.S. appeared in the first two World Cup tournaments in the 1930s and shocked the world by beating England

## BIGGEST WINS IN FINALS 1930-1990

| | |
|---|---|
| 10-1 | Hungary v El Salvador 1982 |
| 9-0 | Hungary v South Korea 1954 |
| | Yugoslavia v Zaire 1974 |
| 8-0 | Sweden v Cuba 1938 |
| | Uruguay v Bolivia 1950 |
| 8-3 | Hungary v West Germany 1954 |
| 7-0 | Turkey v South Korea 1954 |
| | Uruguay v Scotland 1954 |
| | Poland v Haiti 1974 |
| 7-1 | Italy v USA 1934 |
| 7-2 | West Germany v Turkey 1954 |
| 7-3 | France v Paraguay 1958 |
| 7-5 | Austria v Switzerland 1954 |

Note: Austria 7 Switzerland 5 is the highest aggregate for a finals match.

## WORLD CUP FINALS TOURNAMENTS

| Year | Venue | Winners | Runners-up |
|---|---|---|---|
| 1930 | Uruguay | Uruguay | Argentina |
| 1934 | Italy | Italy | Czechoslovakia |
| 1938 | France | Italy | Hungary |
| 1950 | Brazil | Uruguay | Brazil |
| 1954 | Switzerland | West Germany | Hungary |
| 1958 | Sweden | Brazil | Sweden |
| 1962 | Chile | Brazil | Czechoslovakia |
| 1966 | England | England | West Germany |
| 1970 | Mexico | Brazil | Italy |
| 1974 | West Germany | West Germany | Holland |
| 1978 | Argentina | Argentina | Holland |
| 1982 | Spain | Italy | West Germany |
| 1986 | Mexico | Argentina | West Germany |
| 1990 | Italy | West Germany | Argentina |

Gordon Strachan scores Scotland's only goal in the 1986 World Cup finals in Mexico, against West Germany.

1-0 in 1950, but only in the 1990s have we seen a depth of talented American-born players. Let us hope the 1994 World Cup will inspire many more American youngsters to become stars of the 21st century.

So far, in 64 years, 62 nations out of more than twice as many entrants have fought their way to the World Cup finals, but before 1994 only six had won it—Uruguay, Italy, West Germany, Brazil, England and Argentina. We are due for an increase in that last number, as African and Eastern nations add sophistication and organization to the undoubted talents of their athletes. What a spectacle the World Cup might be in 20 years' time! My only regret is that by then I will have hung up my boots. If, however, I am watching a player or two whose fascination for the game began with reading this book, I will be well pleased!

## MOST APPEARANCES IN FINALS 1930-1994

| | | | |
|---|---|---|---|
| 15 | Brazil | | Uruguay |
| 13 | Italy | 8 | Czechoslovakia |
| | West Germany | | Soviet Union |
| | /Germany | | /Russia |
| 11 | Argentina | | Yugoslavia |
| 10 | Mexico | 7 | Scotland |
| 9 | Belgium | | Switzerland |
| | England | 6 | Austria |
| | France | | Bulgaria |
| | Hungary | | Chile |
| | Spain | | Holland |
| | Sweden | | Romania |

Tab Ramos graduated to the senior US World Cup team after playing in the 1983 Under-20 World Cup finals in Mexico.

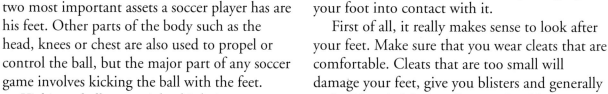

It might be stating the obvious to say that the two most important assets a soccer player has are his feet. Other parts of the body such as the head, knees or chest are also used to propel or control the ball, but the major part of any soccer game involves kicking the ball with the feet.

Kicking a ball, you might think, is a straightforward action that comes naturally—and to most people it does. But if you are to have full control over the ball and make it go where you want it to go and at the right speed, there is more to kicking a soccer ball than merely bringing your foot into contact with it.

First of all, it really makes sense to look after your feet. Make sure that you wear cleats that are comfortable. Cleats that are too small will damage your feet, give you blisters and generally make life painful. Equally, you should not wear cleats that are too big. Once you have found the style or manufacture of cleats which is good for you, my tip is to stick with these cleats all the time.

There are lots of different styles of cleats on the market these days. Some look very flashy and very colorful, but don't be tempted merely by the way the cleats look. It is how they feel when you have them on your feet that counts. I stuck with the same brand of cleats all my career once I found the style that suited me best. Comfort is of chief importance to me and my feet and it should be to you and your feet.

You should ensure that you keep your feet clean and you should make sure that your toenails are not allowed to grow too long or are not cut too short. Either way, they can cause you discomfort and problems.

Having made sure that your feet are in good condition, we come at last to the important part of actually kicking the ball. There are certain points to bear in mind when kicking a soccer ball. Generally speaking, you should not kick the ball with your toes. Use the inside of the foot, the outside or the instep.

The most accurate way of kicking the ball is to use the inside of the foot. As I am right-

I am kicking the ball with the instep, the most used kicking zone. It is the part of the foot which combines power with accuracy and is used for quick free kicks, chips, crosses, long passes, etc.

footed, I use the left side of my right foot to propel the ball and aim it where I would like it to go. Left-footed players would use the right side of their left foot. Of course, if you are "two-footed" then you have a big advantage.

When using the outside of the foot it is difficult to send the ball straight. You will usually find that the ball will "curl" in flight so it is not quite as easy to aim the ball as it is using the inside of the foot. Curling the ball in some situations can be an advantage, however, but this is a skill dealt with later.

The way to get plenty of pace or power on the ball is by kicking it with the top of the foot or instep (the middle section of the foot which forms the arch between the ankle and toes). Goalkeepers use this technique to get the ball downfield and defenders use it to clear an attack. When strikers blast the ball into the net, it is more often than not by using the top of the foot.

It is essential for the good of your game that you try to master the various methods there are of kicking a ball. Certain things are common to them all. Make sure that you keep your eye on the ball all the time. If you are having a shot at goal or passing to a teammate you should have a good idea where the target is without the need for a last-second check, so watch the ball until you have completed your kick.

Finally, it is important to realize the part played by the non-kicking foot. It should be next to the ball when the ball is struck and not ahead of or behind it. This foot determines your balance and the power you can get into the shot.

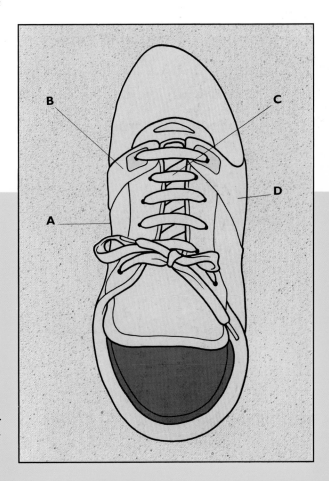

## Kicking area of the foot

**A  The inside:** Used for playing accurate low passes or placing the ball in a specific spot.

**B  The instep:** The most used kicking zone. Chips, crosses, shots of any length can be made with instep.

**C  The top:** The most powerful contact area. A ball driven with the top of the foot will travel with maximum force. This area is used when volleying at goal or clear of trouble.

**D  The outside:** A bending volley, a curving chip or a ball controlling area—that is the role of the outside of the foot.

# PASSING 1

Throughout my career I have always worked on the theory that, no matter how good you may think you are at a certain skill, there is always room for improvement.

I would hate anyone to think I am big-headed but I believe I am blessed with having a good "touch" or "feel" on the ball. Yet this belief has never stopped me in the 20 years I have played the game as a professional from trying to become a better ball passer. Passing is an absolutely basic skill that must be mastered—whatever position you play.

The game is played at a much faster pace these days than it used to be. You are given much less space and very little time on the ball. When I began all those years ago there was a lot more room for errors but that is not the case now. One way that you can get more time to think about

your next move is if you receive an accurate pass that can be quickly controlled.

So you can see that passing needs to be absolutely accurate—and this applies to whatever level you might be playing at. When you find that you can pass the ball accurately it will not only give you a tremendous feeling of satisfaction and enjoyment, you will also have become a far more valuable team member. Your teammates will soon learn to appreciate that a pass from you will arrive where they want it and where they can control it. A ball is much easier to control with the feet—after all we are talking about soccer, not head tennis!

Great passers of the ball are always invaluable members of their teams. After all, it is no good receiving or winning the ball, either as attacker or defender, if you cannot make use of it.

**1** The ball is at my feet and I am shielding it from the defender while I prepare to hit it with the inside of my foot.

**2** Now I have made the pass. Note that the ball is on the ground. Passes along the ground are best because they are easier for the receiver to control than those arriving through the air.

# THE SIDEFOOT PASS

Whenever you can, for shorter distances, use the sidefoot pass. This is the easiest and most accurate method of passing the ball and it allows you to send the ball along the ground while shielding it from your opponent. But always remember your job isn't over when you've made the pass. You must keep the momentum of the movement going. Run into position for a return pass or run into an area where you will be available to continue the attack, or where you will pull a defender off a teammate. Don't stand there admiring yourself but move off quickly and get back in the game!

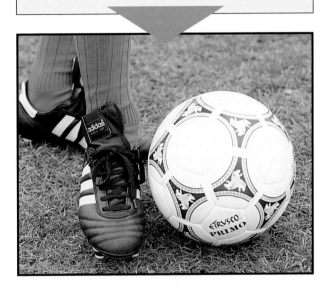

**3** My teammate is now in possession and I have moved forward to open up more free space just in case my teammate wants to use me for a return pass.

## Gordon's GEMS

● When passing, always try to keep yourself between the defender and the ball to give him as little chance as possible of taking the ball from you.

● When tying your laces, make sure the knot is on the top of the foot. If it slips down to the side it can affect the pass when you play the ball sidefooted.

● Don't relax after passing but move into an open area and keep in the game.

# PASSING 2

## CHIP PASS

I like to think of the chip as an attacking skill because it can be used to score a goal, beat a defensive "wall" or put a teammate into an attacking position. It can open up the tightest-marking defenses. But it can also be used if you are under pressure in a defensive situation.

Both the outside and the inside of the foot—as well as the top—can be used when you chip the ball, but to play this difficult pass with a reasonable degree of accuracy you must practice long and hard. Even if you think you are blessed with skills, there is still a need to work at this aspect of your game.

The chip can be very rewarding, as one of its main uses is in scoring goals by lifting the ball over the goalkeeper's head if he happens to be out of position too far off his line.

### TECHNIQUE

The way to play the chip shot is to "stab" at the ball and get your foot underneath it, as you see me doing in the picture below. Contact is made with the lower part of the instep and this has the effect of putting backspin on the ball and making it float away. There should be only a short back-lift of the kicking leg and hardly any follow-through when making this pass.

## Gordon's GEMS

● Where possible, I prefer to use the more easily controlled ground pass to the more ambitious chip pass, reserving the chip for occasions when the less risky ground pass is blocked.

● When you make up your mind that you are going to chip, make the pass confidently and you will have a better chance of playing it well.

● Don't give your opponent a chance of intercepting the pass. Make sure you chip the ball high enough over his head.

**1** As I prepare to kick the ball, my head is nearly over it. I take care not to get my head too far forward or I will not be able to get the ball up high enough.

**2** My kicking foot has come through and lifted the ball into the air but my eyes are still fixed on the ball. Taking your eye off the ball is fatal for any passing move.

**3** I lean back slightly to see the ball pass high over the defender on its way to my teammate. Only now have I permitted myself to watch the result of the pass.

**4** The ball is landing at the feet of my teammate, while the opponent is helpless. It is satisfying to see the ball obey my wishes. A job well done!

# PASSING 3

## BENDING THE BALL

One of the points which I will keep stressing in this book is the need to practice. I make no apologies for repeating this. In my view there is no such thing as the perfect soccer player but practice is a valuable aid in helping you to achieve your potential no matter at what level you may be playing the game.

If you are right-footed, as I am, and you use the outside of your foot to "graze" the left half of the ball it should curve away to the right (if you are left-footed and use this particular method the ball will curve to the left). Should you decide to use the inside of your foot to "graze" the right half of the ball it will curve away to the left. (The opposite will apply if you are left-footed.)

When you make this shot or pass make sure that the non-kicking foot is in line with the ball and that you follow through with the kicking foot the same way a golfer does when he drives a ball off the tee.

### TECHNIQUE

Keep your eyes on the ball and with the outside of your kicking foot make contact with the side of the ball. It is vital in making this pass that you follow through with the kicking leg. If you have done this correctly then the ball should spin as it goes through the air and this in turn makes the ball "curve" on its way to the player who is due to receive the ball. Once you have mastered this technique you can use it to very good effect during games — it is one of the most effective ways of causing your opponents problems.

## Gordon's GEMS

● Make sure you exaggerate the follow-through with your kicking leg when making this pass.

● This is not an easy pass to make, so practice it as often as you can.

● Do not under-hit this pass. One of the most frustrating things in the game is to lose the ball because the strength of the pass is wrong.

**1** A defender is ready to challenge, so I decide to "bend" the ball around him to my teammate on the wing. As you can see I have followed through with the foot after striking the ball.

**2** The ball "curves" around the challenging player and towards the winger who moved forward to meet it as soon as he saw my intention.

**3** The winger has managed to receive my pass ahead of the defender without being tackled, and he is ready to take the ball down the wing or pass inside.

# *PASSING 4*

## THE WALL PASS

There are various ways in which you can attempt to beat an opponent—one of the most effective being the "wall," or "screen," pass. This gets you past him without the need to dribble, and is much easier and less risky than dribbling.

In effect, you use a teammate as if he were a wall, passing the ball to him and collecting the "rebound." As with most things in soccer, timing is of the greatest importance. I first learned this particular move as a rookie by watching a couple of guys who were very good at it. I soon realized how effective the move can be.

It is easy to use, provided you time it right. If you are too far away from the defender when you attempt the wall pass, then the defender has the time to turn and win possession. If you are too close, the defender can stick out a leg to intercept or deflect the pass. Time it correctly, and a defender preparing to tackle you finds you running past him without the ball. There is nothing he can do.

Of course, you need to have a teammate in a good position to receive and return the ball to you as you run on to take the pass.

Opponents do not stand about like dummies while you execute your pretty moves around them, so it is necessary to catch the defender flat-footed. You do this with a swift change of pace. While the defender is reacting, turning and taking up the chase, your sudden sprint forward should leave him far behind.

When I was a youngster I was known as a dribbler, but when I turned professional I soon learned the value of passing. I was straight out of school and eager to learn and make a career playing soccer. I soon found what a help it was to study older and more experienced players. You

**1** I make a determined run at the defender and just as I get near to him I pass the ball to my teammate who is in a forward position.

**2** Once the pass has been made and the ball is on the way to my teammate I accelerate and make a run forward myself.

should listen to any advice coaches and teammates may have to offer. You can decide afterwards whether their advice feels right for you personally, but you have nothing to lose by listening and a great deal to gain.

As a rookie, I nursed an ambition that one day during a game I would make two successive wall passes on my way to scoring a goal. But it was many years before I managed it. In a run from the half way line I played three wall passes and finished off by shooting, with my left foot. To this day I think that was the best goal I have ever scored. I probably ran half the length of the field, had four touches on the ball and scored—which just goes to show the value of the wall pass. It saves a lot of running with the ball and can pay a rich dividend. But the angle of the pass, the speed of the ball and the touch from the target man—the "wall"—has to be right, as has the timing of your run.

## Gordon's GEMS

● It is essential that your pass is accurate if you are to make the most of what is a very productive move.

● Increasing your pace is a must if your marker is to be caught flat-footed.

● Make sure the ball is played wide enough to prevent the defender sticking out a leg to block the ball.

● Be alert to the possibility of acting as a "wall" yourself for one of your teammates carrying the ball forward.

**3** My teammate takes up possession and immediately knocks the ball into the area that I am running into behind the defender.

**4** The defender has been caught flat-footed. Having moved forward, I am ready to take the ball again and carry it toward the goal.

# THE FIRST TOUCH 1

When a player always seems to find room to move in and never seems rushed, it usually comes down to the fact that the player's first touch on the ball is a good one and he is able to control the ball quickly even when receiving a poor pass.

As I often say, time and space are rare commodities in the modern game when defenders are so fit and fast. A good first touch can allow you that time and space. It might only be a second or two but that is all you need to be able to get a good pass away, turn a defender or take a snap shot.

As far as I am concerned, initial control is one of the easier skills to learn. Once you feel comfortable about receiving the ball from any angle, you can develop this skill to a higher level. Then, instead of the ball's bouncing away from you when you receive it from a teammate, you can take it and, in one movement, swivel around to face the way you want to go rather than have to use maybe as many as three touches to make the turn.

I learned to do this as a student by kicking the ball for hours and hours against two walls at right angles to each other, and even when I became a professional I used this very basic method to continue to improve my skills. All you need are the two walls and a ball—and, of course, the determination and patience to be prepared to put in plenty of practice. The method is simple and effective.

What you do is kick the ball against one wall and when it comes back turn and hit it against the other wall. Do this with your feet, head or other parts of the body. Keep on doing it non-stop for about 20 minutes and you will probably get over 1,000 touches on the ball. This is the beauty of the method because it is impossible to get that number of touches on the

ball by playing 80 or 90 minutes in a soccer game. You will find that the concentrated effort also helps build up your stamina and concentration. The more you improve, the more you'll enjoy it.

## TRAPPING THE BALL

The trap is a fundamental method of controlling a bouncing ball. I get my foot high to bring it down on the ball.

# CONTROLLING THE BALL WITH THE INSIDE OF THE LEG

**1** The ball is bouncing towards me and I let it hit the inside of my raised leg. I ride the ball back slightly along the line of flight to bring it under control.

**2** After hitting my leg the ball drops to the ground and I am in control of it, ready to do whatever I want with it.

If you can get your initial control of the ball— the first touch—right, then you will have gone a long way toward being an effective player. Your confidence will grow when you know you can receive a ball from any direction.

On the other hand, if you do not master this particular skill, you could struggle in today's game because players are specifically coached to keep opponents from playing the ball, to "close them down." If you cannot trap a ball properly and control it quickly, such players will blot you out of the game by marking up tight and stepping in to take the ball as soon as you let it slip out of your control.

## CONTROLLING ON THE CHEST

One of the most important points to bear in mind when attempting to control the ball with your chest is to be relaxed. I would far rather try to control the ball with the chest than to head it. That might have something to do with the fact that I have never been able to head the ball all that well! But the chest is, after all, a large and safe area on which to control the soccer ball.

As with heading, you must keep your eyes firmly fixed on the ball. As it comes towards you through the air, try to pick up the flight and anticipate where it will drop.

Watching closely, move into a good position and be up on your toes and leaning back slightly as the ball makes contact with your chest. Try to "cushion" the impact or allow it to hit you naturally.

When the ball hits your chest it will then begin to drop and the quicker you gain control with your feet the better. It is important that you complete this movement smoothly and quickly.

If you are a defender and an attacker is closing in on you it is possible for you to deflect the ball away from him by turning the chest as the ball hits it, dropping the ball to one side.

**1** I am up on my toes and leaning back slightly as the ball drops onto my chest.

**2** The ball is on a downward path and I am about to let it hit my raised leg.

**3** Now the ball is down at my feet and that's where I like it. Control is better there.

**1** The ball is on its way to me and I make sure I watch it closely.

**2** The leg I am using to control the ball is angled down and that's also the direction in which I am looking.

**3** he ball is on the ground and I am already passing it on.

# CONTROLLING ON THE THIGH

The technique for taking control of the ball on the thigh is much the same as that for controlling it on the chest.

You will make a mess of it, however, unless you follow the flight of the ball closely. As the ball arrives, you need to be in position with your thigh at an angle of about 45 degrees to the ground. Watch the ball right onto your thigh. When it hits your thigh it will bounce down and you then need to be ready to keep the game flowing, either by immediately moving off with the ball at your feet or by playing it to a teammate.

Speed of thought and action are vital ingredients in soccer and if you can complete this particular move smoothly and swiftly, so much the better.

## Gordon's GEMS

● Keeping your eyes on the ball is vital when controlling the ball with your chest or thigh.

● It is important to be relaxed. The ball is hard but it will not hurt when it hits the chest or thigh.

● Execute these moves swiftly and you will often avoid being tackled or bumped around.

● When bringing the ball down make sure your raised leg is angled down; otherwise the ball will bounce back up from your knee and you will lose tight control.

## CONTROLLING WITH THE HEAD AND PASSING ON

I have to be honest and confess that heading the ball is not one of the stronger points in my game. I have managed to score quite a lot of goals in my career but I think that in 21 years of playing I managed to score only four with my head.

However, I certainly admire those players who can head the ball well. Such players are not all really tall, but their timing is excellent, and that is the secret of being a good ball header.

Heading is not just a matter of scoring goals or clearing from defense—sometimes a pass will come to you head-high, and you will have to bring it under control, move off with it yourself or aim a controlled head pass to a teammate.

Once you have decided to use your head to control the ball, you must keep your eye on the ball, be positive and not allow yourself to be deflected from what you intend to do by the closeness of opponents.

The front part of your forehead is where you should make contact with the ball. Obviously you must keep your eyes open to ensure you connect properly. Remember that the skull is tough and a properly headed ball does not hurt.

Before making contact you must know just what you are going to do and in which direction you want to move once the ball has arrived. As the ball hits your head try to "cushion" the blow and at the point of impact turn slightly in the direction you wish the ball to move.

Do not jump unnecessarily. Some players jump when just as good a contact could be made if they stayed on their feet. Then they would be able to move off quickly into a new position.

These days, with space on the ground at a premium because of crowded midfields and penalty areas, some teams use "target men" to whom the ball is passed in the air and whose job it is to flick it on or knock it down for a teammate. Many goals are scored this way, so it can be seen that control with the head is a vital part of the game.

Controlling the ball with the head is often overlooked by defenders who see their role primarily as clearing the ball from the danger area and getting the ball as far upfield as possible. However, a defender aware of the positions of his teammates, and who can direct his header toward one of them, will perform a much greater service for his side. Instead of clearing into "no-man's land," where the ball might quickly be returned by the opposition, he can initiate an attack by his own team.

## Gordon's GEMS

● Concentration is again the name of the game—keep your eye on the ball.

● Make up your mind about what you are going to do with the ball and be positive.

● Balance is important, so make sure you are relaxed and not leaning too far forward.

**1** As the ball comes to me I position myself so that I can jump and allow the ball to make contact with my forehead.

**2** When I head the ball I turn my head slightly at the same time to enable me to aim the ball in the direction of my teammate.

**3** My teammate is about to take possession and I begin to move forward so that I am ready if he wants to pass back to me.

# PLAYING IN ATTACK

**B**ecause most goals are scored by players who play attack positions, these are usually seen as the most glamorous. Everyone loves players who score goals and as far as I am concerned there is no finer feeling in the game than scoring a goal.

Strikers come in all shapes and sizes, and employ different methods, but what is common to them all, of course, is a hunger and an eye for a goal. Pace, height, strength and confidence are also useful assets, as well as a willingness to take the sort of knocks that occur when

Mick Harford is a perfect example of the tall, strong "target man" who spreads panic amongst defenders.

everybody is going all out in the penalty area.

Not all strikers are extremely athletic. A different type of striker is what we call the "target man," a less mobile player who specializes in getting open for teammates to cross the ball to. He is a midfield player's dream because he makes himself so readily available, and his strength and sheer determination make him a major problem for defenders.

A target man can take a lot of knocks from big defenders as he waits for balls to be played in from the flanks or midfield. If this role appeals to you, obviously you will need to be big and strong to compete with them.

In addition to scoring goals yourself, if you are a target man you should also try to create scoring opportunities for teammates by knocking balls down to those running into the penalty area or six-yard box.

Strikers are the kings of the six-yard box when they are alert to scoring opportunities and quick in their ability to get the ball into the net. If this is your role you cannot relax. You must always be concentrating, always trying to anticipate the unexpected and always on your toes ready to pounce. Your main asset is your ability to get two steps on slower-witted defenders.

Attackers who play on the flanks are known as wings or outside forwards or, as I have been referred to, as wide receivers. Outside forwards used to wait for the ball to be played to them, but today the men who play "wide" are expected to attack, defend and often go in search of the ball. If you want to be a wide player today, you must be prepared to put in a lot of running.

Remember that, although the strike force is where individual skills possibly count the most, even here soccer is still a team game. The wing might beat his man every time and make dazzling runs down the sideline, but his work will come to nothing if nobody is available in the middle to convert it into goals. It is no good for a target man to lose his marker, or a mobile striker to burst clear in the penalty area or make a diagonal run, if nobody passes the ball to him.

The beauty of being a striker is that you can improvise, you can take up unusual positions, you can attempt the ambitious and the unexpected. It doesn't matter if most of the time nothing comes of your enterprise. If you try 20 moves in a game and two succeed, leading to

A more complete player than the pure "target man," Alan Shearer is quick and skillful.

Perhaps the greatest modern day center forward, Holland's Marco Van Basten, is big but skillful . . . and a clinical finisher.

your scoring two goals, you will be a hero, and nobody will care about the 18 times you attempted something which didn't work.

Although the striker is always trying to make things happen by upsetting the routine, he must be prepared to help out elsewhere on the field, and even occasionally to defend. Then his job is to be reliable and consistent. If he makes two errors which lead to goals his offensive flair will be small consolation.

Be aware of the needs of the team. If the fullback sprints down the wing the wide man should cover for him. If a midfielder makes a break down the center, the central strikers should support him by drawing off defenders or making themselves available.

The strikers get most of the glory—it is only fair they share the work!

# SHOOTING AT GOAL 1

## SHOOTING AT GOAL FROM CLOSE RANGE

When you are shooting from close range, it is essential that you make your shot on target. There is nothing worse than seeing somebody blast the ball from six yards out, only for it to go past the wrong side of the post or over the bar. Admittedly it is great to see the ball crashing into the back of the net. All youngsters love to see that happen, especially when playing with proper nets for the first time.

But it is not always necessary to blast the ball in, as all top strikers will readily tell you. You will find as much enjoyment and satisfaction from sidefooting the ball or merely tapping it into the goal, when that is really all that is needed to score a goal. And of course a controlled tap cuts down the chance of accidents. If, as the ball comes across the goal, you are unlucky enough to get a bad bounce or a bobble at the last minute, you then have that split second to adjust because, by shaping up for a tap-in, you have more control over your movement than if you were just going to smash the ball.

Of course, many close-in goals (like the majority of mine!) are scored by instinct and reflex action. Your foot seems to move to score without any conscious thought on your part. But

**1** Photographed from the back of the net, I have knocked the ball forward and have managed to get away from the defender.

**2** My run is timed so that I meet the ball with the inside of my favored right foot to enable me to score with a sidefoot shot.

if you think about most of the close-in goals scored, the common factor is that the scorer was always in the right position. Anticipation is what leads to many close-range goals. Always be alert to what is going on and what might happen next. Take nothing for granted. Always have rebounds in mind. Try to guess where the ball might go and get there too!

Always be ready to try a shot when close to goal and do not mind if you miss. Even the best strikers miss a lot. One goal makes up for a dozen near-misses.

Strikers should develop a mind-set where it is natural to do things early. Hesitation is the greatest crime when a close-in chance arises. So cultivate an attitude where you don't need to think—as soon as the ball arrives, you act.

I still find it as great a thrill scoring a goal now as I did when I first came into the game as a teenager many years ago. The fun of scoring always makes all the hard work and knocks that preceded it seem worthwhile.

When I find myself in position for a close range shot—and by close range I mean somewhere about eight yards from goal—I try to remain cool, calm and collected and go for placement and a controlled strike. There is nothing to be gained from panicking, and going for a really hard strike can cut down on accuracy and control.

From my own experience of scoring goals from close range I have also found that the best chance of beating the goalkeeper is by hitting the ball along the ground.

**3** The ball is on its way into the net. The job is done and I am turning away to celebrate!

# Gordon's GEMS

● When trying to beat the goalkeeper, aim low. A shot at his waist level is easier for him to save than one on the ground.

● Don't panic in front of goal. Remain calm and make sure you get your shot on target.

● Never blast the ball when there is no need to. You have more control over the ball if you are not trying to blast it.

## LONG-RANGE SHOOTING

Because there is so much good defensive play nowadays, especially by teams who push out quickly to play offside, it is necessary to score a good percentage of goals by long-range shooting.

Long-range shooting really needs only the application of basic kicking skills. If you can kick powerfully, then you can shoot from long range. The added requirement, perhaps, is an awareness of the situation and quick thinking. Defenders are always trying to close strikers down to prevent their getting in a shot—the striker's job therefore is to outwit them and take the defense (including the goalkeeper) by surprise.

A long-range shot, unless it's a chip, should be powerful. For maximum power, the non-kicking leg should be alongside the ball at the moment of impact, the head directly over the ball. The top of the foot imparts most force to a kick, but you cannot always choose the optimum position for shooting. You might be forced to volley or half-volley, or strike the ball with the instep or outside of the foot, or be forced to shoot with an opponent bearing down on you.

The main requirement is that, once you have decided to shoot, do it with conviction and confidence. Keep your eye on the ball and follow through after hitting it.

Just because you are further away from the goal, do not think that there is less chance of a surprise shot than when you are close in. In some ways, surprise is more important. A good goalkeeper will not be beaten easily from way out—surprising him gives you a better chance.

Obviously, you must try hard to get your shots on target, although I accept that there is a greater margin for error compared to shots from close range. Errors and mishaps can work in your favor, however. The shot may be deflected or the goalkeeper's vision may be blocked.

It is surprisingly difficult to hit the ball hard over a long distance without its swerving a little. Of course a swerve on a powerful long shot improves the chance of beating the goalkeeper. You can deliberately put swerve on your shot by using the technique of bending the ball explained on page 16. If you can get power, swerve and direction, you have a good chance of scoring.

When shooting from a long distance you must aim for one of the corners of the goal. The best goalkeepers are rarely beaten by a long shot which is close to them. You have to accept that not every long-range shot you attempt will be on target but my message to all budding long-range artists is: "Don't be afraid to miss."

## Gordon's GEMS

● When trying a long-range shot don't be afraid of missing. Nothing ventured, nothing gained!

● Try to aim for one of the corners of the goal—it makes it more difficult for the goalkeeper to get to the ball.

● Make up your mind and go for it. Never change your mind as you prepare to shoot.

**1** Defenders are closing in fast and I haven't the pace to get away so I choose to try my luck with a shot at goal.

**2** The goalkeeper is more to one side of the goal so I've aimed for the other side.

**3** The defenders are on me but they're too late. The goalkeeper has made a valiant attempt but it's another goal for me!

# SHOOTING AT GOAL 3

One of the most satisfying goals of my career, scored for Scotland against Romania in 1986. Their goalkeeper had strayed off his line and I left him stranded with a lob from the edge of the box.

## CHIPPING THE GOALKEEPER

A particularly satisfying way to score is with the chip shot or lob, using the same technique described earlier for the chip pass.

You have to be positive in a situation like this, so once you have made up your mind you are going to attempt the chip, don't change it. Stick to that course of action.

When the goalkeeper comes off his line and advances towards you, the opportunity is there for you to "lift" or chip the ball high enough over his head so that he cannot reach it, but with only enough force on the ball to allow it to drop behind him and into the net.

**1** The ball is at my feet and I notice that the goalkeeper has advanced off his line.

**2** I have chipped the ball high in the air, over the defenders, and it's on its way to goal.

# ONLY THE GOALKEEPER TO BEAT

When you suddenly find yourself in a one-on-one situation with the goalkeeper you are faced with making a quick decision.

If you choose to try a shot on the run remember to hit the ball low and hard. It is often a help to glance at the goalkeeper when you are about ten yards from him. You will usually find he has come out to narrow the angle.

Should that be the case, a split second or so before you shoot, touch the ball slightly to one side. This tends to put the goalkeeper off and you will have a better chance of beating him.

I remember one one-on-one situation against a goalkeeper who could be a bit of an eccentric at times. He stood there glaring at me but I kept cool and made up my mind what I was going to do. I chose the option of hitting the ball close to his feet. I think that if I had put it more to his side he might have got to the ball.

Anyway I succeeded and scored what was our equalizer and, believe me, it was a very satisfying moment for me!

Another way of beating the goalkeeper is to pretend you are going to fire into one corner by looking that particular way and, when the goalkeeper (you hope!) moves to anticipate you, you suddenly change direction and hit it into the other corner.

If instead of standing up, the goalkeeper begins to dive at your feet you can often chip the ball over him. But try not to let the goalkeeper get too close to you, as the nearer he gets the better his chance of smothering the ball.

**3** The goalkeeper sees the ball, realizes he is off his line and begins to move back.

**4** He has made a desperate effort to retrace his steps but it is too late. The ball has cleared him and dipped in under the bar.

# DRIBBLING AND CLOSE CONTROL 1

**M**any people would say dribbling is a dying art but really it should not be, as it's a skill that fans love to see and defenders don't!

In this age of tight marking and solid defenses, there is nothing better than watching a player who can dribble his way past opponents. It is also extremely effective.

## DEVELOPING THE CUT AWAY

There will be many times during a game when you find yourself face to face with a defender or an opponent in a one-on-one situation. You have to make up your mind quickly whether you are going to pass to a teammate who may be in a better position and not so closely marked—or decide to take on the defender and beat him.

If you decide on (or are forced into) the second option, the "cut away" move is one way in which you can beat your opponent.

You have the ball at your feet and you are making progress. Everything is going well and then suddenly you discover a defender blocking your path and moving in to challenge you.

A key to beating this opponent with the "cut away" is confidence and good control. As you get to him, throw your right foot past the ball (if you are right-footed, that is) and with the outside of the foot drag the ball back. You will find that your momentum will carry you past the ball a little. Turn your body to the right to shield the ball from him and move away.

In effect you have gone up to the defender and "cut away" from him—hence the name we give to this particular movement. You can practice this move initially on your own, but the best way of practicing it is with a friend, as the pictures on the opposite page show.

The "cut away" is similar in some respects to the "cut," which I will explain in detail later in the book. For the "cut" you approach the defender and then using the inside of your right foot "cut" the ball to the inside.

With the "cut away" you buy yourself a second or so of time and a yard or two of space—enough to open up more options for your next move.

*Gordon's* **GEMS**

● You must keep close to the ball when attempting the "cut away" move.

● Practice this move five minutes a day with your friend—you'll be amazed how it improves your game.

● Try practicing this move using your weaker foot too, e.g., turn to the left instead of the right (as the center player is doing in the pictures).

**1** The attacker has a ball at his feet and sets off running towards the defender at three-quarter pace.

**2** When the attacker is near the defender, he throws his right foot past the ball in order to drag it back in the direction from which he came.

**3** At the same time the attacker's momentum carries him past the ball, he turns his body to present his back to the defender.

**4** The attacker nearest the camera is perfectly positioned. His body is completely shielding the ball from the defender and he has it under control as he moves away.

# DRIBBLING AND
# CLOSE CONTROL 2

## THE CROSSOVER FAKE

The crossover fake is probably as well known, if not better known, as "the Rivelino move," named after the famous midfield player of the Brazilian World Cup–winning team in Mexico back in 1970. Everyone knew he would use this move at some time or other, but he executed it so well that opponents found it virtually impossible to keep their balance when he did so.

As in the "cut," or the "Cruyff turn" which I describe later, it does not necessarily have to beat the opponent. The intention is to confuse him and buy a little time while keeping you and your team in possession.

The crossover fake is not a skill that I have in my locker. Believe me, I wish I had, but unfortunately it is something I never practiced when I was younger. Young readers should note that practicing the various skills is better done now. For an old player like myself, practicing something new can be uncomfortable. It certainly does not come as easily as it might have done years earlier, so take my tip and master the skills as best you can when you are young.

When you use the crossover fake you are trying to trick the defender into wrongly thinking you are going to kick the ball forward.

You throw your kicking foot over the ball, unbalancing the defender. Make sure the outside of the foot is alongside the ball. Then drag the ball back. You are then able to move off in a different direction leaving the defender on the

wrong foot and struggling to recover. At its best, this maneuver buys you a second or two of time to set up an attack.

On the page opposite is my favorite exercise for developing "the Rivelino." Four players are shown practicing the move with me as a defender in the middle. Practicing in groups like this, particularly if there is a coach to help and direct your efforts, is a big advantage, as it helps you gauge your progress and you can encourage each other. But don't lose sight of the object of the exercise, which is practice!

## Gordon's GEMS

● After eight attempts at this movement, change the man in the middle and carry on.

● When throwing the kicking foot past the ball, really exaggerate the move. Make the defender react.

● Take it easy when practicing. It is not necessary to dash about. Polish is more important than pace.

**1** Four players, each with a ball, jog towards the defender in the middle.

**2** As they arrive at the defender they throw their right foot past the ball, placing it at the side of the ball.

**3** With the outside of the foot the attackers now take the ball at right angles away from the defender.

**4** They now take the ball towards the next cone, ready to face the defender and practice the move all over again.

# BEATING YOUR OPPONENT 1

## THE FEINT

Every player, including defenders, should be able to dribble with the ball because this is a skill which can always be put to good use. But it is a skill which does not come easily to the majority of players, so once again practice is a must.

All you need is a ball and a bit of space. Run with the ball at your feet, sometimes quickly and sometimes a little slower. When you feel comfortable with the ball at your feet, set up a line of obstacles, ideally cones, but anything will do, and weave your way between them as if they were opponents, keeping the ball as close to your toe as possible. Use both feet, and both the instep and outside of the foot, until you are confident you can control the ball in tight situations. Keep at it and eventually you will get the "feel" of the ball and become a better player.

Once you are able to control the ball in this way you are ready to add another skill to your repertoire—the feint. Basically, the feint is used for changing direction. It is a close-control move for making defenders lose balance and is the most used move in the game by players who are in possession of the ball.

With the feint, you approach the defender with the ball at your toes and convince him that you intend to go one way, thus getting him

**1** The defender has done his job and slowed me down by his challenge. I decide to use the feint.

**2** Making sure the ball is not too far from my foot, I feint as if about to play the ball with my right instep, and move to the left.

**3** Here the defender begins to lose his balance as he goes too far to his right and I begin to move away with the ball, using the outside of my right foot.

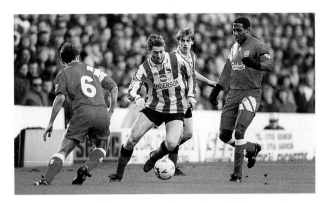

it can buy you time and space on the ball by keeping him from tackling you. This skill is a "must" for players who want to excel, especially those who play in attack.

Look closely at Chris Waddle, shown executing the feint in the photograph above, and you will see that he really exaggerates the movement. You know what he is going to do. You swear you won't buy it during the game but, of course, you fall for it just as you have in the past and you are left sprawling in the grass.

The feint is often used by wide players against fullbacks. Feinting to come inside, they will sprint past the fullback on the outside and head for the end line.

When faced with a forward with the ball at his toes, a defender's first thought will be not to commit himself too hastily to the tackle. If he lunges in and is beaten he has no chance to recover, so his first object will be to keep his feet. It is better for the defender to retreat than to be beaten in a tackle, and an astute defender, by his positioning, can sometimes force the attacker to go the way he wants, allowing his teammates to group accordingly.

unbalanced while you go the other. The usual feint is to pretend to play the ball with the instep but actually to use the outside of the foot to go around the defender on his other side. If it is perfectly timed and executed, the defender takes so long to change direction that you are in the clear.

The more you use this when you are younger, the more attuned to the movement your body will become. It is harder when you are older and your body is not so supple.

To make the most of the feint, you need to overemphasize your first movement. A good first move will tend to unbalance the defender and, though you may not get by him with one move,

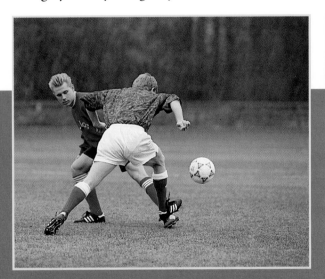

**4** From a crouching position I decide to lift the ball over the foot of the defender's outstretched left leg with the outside of my right foot.

**5** The defender has blown his chance and I dart away still in possession of the ball. He has to turn and cannot prevent me from gaining several yards on him.

# BEATING YOUR OPPONENT 2

## THE CUT

This is probably my favorite move in soccer—especially when I am going down the left side of the field. I have been making good use of this move for a long, long time—as long as I can remember, in fact.

My liking for this particular move probably has something to do with the fact that it is one of the easiest to perform!

I remember years ago playing against the team of one of my best friends and I knew he wanted the players on his side not to fall for the Gordon Strachan "cut." He knew I loved the move and would at, some stage of the game, bring it into use. Very early, I got away on the left flank and as I ran towards the defender I made it look as if I were going to play the ball to the middle of the field. At the last moment, I "cut" the ball back and went away down the flank.

The defender had bought it and only five minutes of the game had gone. I could hear my friend screaming at his defender, but the fact is that although this move is relatively simple and easy to do it is not one that is easy to defend against.

For some reason shorter players like myself are particularly good at this move, perhaps because we are closer to the ball and can turn quicker than more cumbersome defenders.

When you play the "cut" you have to be confident and feel comfortable on the ball and not be worried about failing. On occasions the defender will stop you, but it is worth remembering that the defender has a difficult job

if you execute the move correctly.

And, of course, once the defender has committed himself and you are past him, he has no chance to recover. You have effectively cut your marker out of the game and bought precious seconds to set up an attack.

The "cut" can be useful when you are near the corner flag, covered by a defender. A move as if you were going to center the ball will commit the defender into attempting a block, and you can "cut" the ball past him. Some players use the maneuver in this situation to switch the ball to their stronger foot. But do not overdo it, or the defense will get wise.

## Gordon's GEMS

- Shout at a teammate in the middle of the field as though you are thinking of passing to him.

- Always exaggerate the first movement with the kicking leg.

- Increase your pace once the defender has fallen for the trick.

**1** Looking down at the ball I try to make it look as if I am going to kick the ball into the middle of the field.

**2** The defender stretches in an attempt to stop the pass, but as my foot comes down I change direction and "cut" the ball to the left, using the inside of my foot.

**3** The defender is now completely off balance. He's beaten and I have pushed the ball away at right angles.

# BEATING YOUR OPPONENT 3

## THE "CRUYFF" TURN

When I was beginning my career as a professional soccer player, Johan Cruyff was taking over from Pele as the game's most exciting player. I think of him at his peak somewhere around the 1974 World Cup finals. Holland, whom Cruyff captained, were undoubtedly the team with the most flair and everybody's favorites, but they didn't quite click in the final and lost to West Germany.

Every player in that Dutch team from the fullbacks to the forwards had excellent skills on the ball and it was said that each of them could play virtually any position on the field. Even on this team, Cruyff's dribbling skills stood out. I particularly remember one move with which, three or four times during that tournament, he completely bamboozled his marker. To the spectator it looked almost like a conjuring trick and became known as the "Cruyff turn." Many players have tried to incorporate it into their game and succeeded in making it work, but none manages it with quite the same breathtaking skill as Cruyff.

**1** I have lifted my right leg as if to strike the ball, and the opponent has moved to block the kick.

**2** I am cutting the ball behind my standing foot with my right instep.

The move is basically used to change direction, sending the marker one way while you take the ball the other way. It can be used to create space to take the ball across goal for a shot, or it can be used down the wings when the marker is preventing you from cutting in or denying you space for a pass or cross.

Your opponent is beaten by selling him a fake and by playing the ball behind your standing leg—not exactly a backheel but the nearest you will come to dribbling around your man with a backheel!

It is a spectacular skill but, like everything else, there is a time and place for it. If you have the will to practice it and perfect it, don't get carried away with it. Keep the element of surprise, and use it in a game only where it will make you most dangerous, or when there is no simpler alternative.

As with all skills, execute the move with confidence. Don't be afraid you will trip over your legs and look a fool.

This maneuver, performed quickly and expertly, can demoralize an opponent. But it is a skill quite unlike any other in the game, and it will work only if executed properly. If you bungle it or perform it too slowly, it will look as if you had changed your mind in mid-dribble and you will lose control of the ball. So practice it well in training before using it in a game.

## Gordon's GEMS

● Your opponent must believe that you are about to strike the ball, so make an exaggerated fake to kick it.

● You can use your instep or the bottom of your toes to bring the ball back behind your standing leg.

● Accelerate away from your opponent—don't give him a chance to recover!

**3** I quickly turn inside my opponent, who is now completely wrong-footed and going in the wrong direction.

**4** I accelerate away to the left, leaving the opponent going the wrong way.

# PLAYING IN MIDFIELD

**P**laying in midfield is a very demanding area of the game—I know that from 20 years' experience playing there!

Basically, you can put midfield players into two categories—the first being what I would term a creative one, a category where I would like to think I belong. Secondly, there are those players who go in determined to win the ball, in which category I definitely do not include myself! Nowadays these players are known as "ball-winners."

In my view, one of the most complete creative midfield players over the last 15 years was Glenn Hoddle. He played equally well with either foot and could hit short passes and long passes with almost equal accuracy. He could score great goals and generally he looked a very elegant player all the time. I have always been a bit envious of him because of that!

If you wish to become one of the great ball-winners—players who go in not merely to stop an opponent with a tackle but to come out of that tackle with the ball—then you need look no further than David Batty. David is brave and fearless in the tackle and is also skillful enough that when he comes away with the ball he has the ability to set another attack going.

If I say that the main role of a midfield player is as a support player, I am not talking down the role. In fact, you could say the opposite, because the complete midfielder has to be good at many things. He must support the defense—falling back, covering, making himself available for a pass from the back—and he must support the attack—providing support for the man with the ball, giving him options, drawing defenders, even running from deep to become a striker himself. And of course he must support his fellow midfielders, because the midfield players form the "engine-room" of the team which makes things happen.

In these days of sophisticated formations, it is often difficult for strikers to find space in heavily defended areas around the penalty spot, and the midfielder will sometimes be required to act as a winger, overlapping the forwards to get deep into opponents' territory and pull a defender or two away from the center. When the opponents are

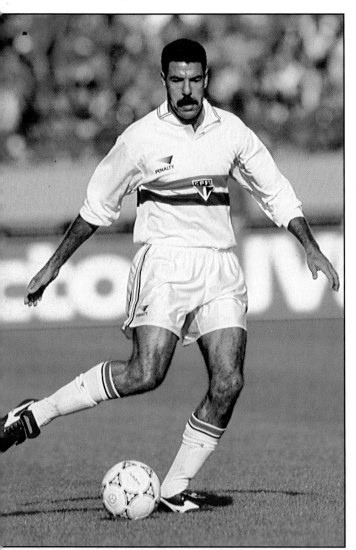

One of the best midfielders I ever played against—Toninho Cerezo of Brazil.

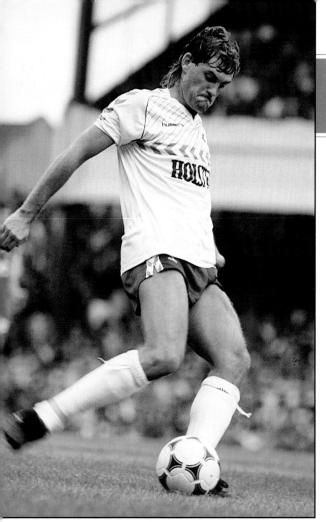

Glenn Hoddle always seemed unhurried on the ball and was a very accurate passer with either foot. He could also rifle in some superb long-range shots.

in midfield, as there are all sorts of midfielders around you for you to base your game upon. My advice is to discover your own strengths and develop them, but also to work on your weaknesses. Your coach and teammates will always admire you if you can do some things really well, but in midfield you cannot afford to do anything really badly.

employing an offside trap, i.e., the defense are moving up in unison to catch the strikers offside, he will be expected to make long runs from his own half to catch the defense unawares and disrupt their tactics.

Of course, the opposing midfield will be employing similar tactics, so he must also be prepared to double back and cover his own defenders. This is where the defensive side of the role becomes uppermost—he most get in his tackles and try to win the ball back.

Today the midfielder needs to have it all—he must have limitless stamina and the enthusiasm to cover most of the field; he must also have pace, vision, ball control, a tackle and a shot.

A tall order! But no need to despair. As I mentioned earlier, there is a chance to specialize

A tireless midfield ball-winner, David Batty also has the passing skills to set attacks going.

# ADVANCED

# SHOOTING SKILLS 1

There is nothing quite like the thrill of volleying the ball into the back of the net from 25 yards. It is not perhaps surprising that this skill is one which most people seem to love to practice, whether they are beginners or professionals.

A player volleys the ball when he kicks it before it has a chance to hit the ground. In other words he hits the ball while it is still in flight and, because you can swing the full weight of your body into this shot, the volley is regarded as the hardest or strongest method of striking the ball. It is a great thrill when you hit the ball clearly and it flies from your foot—but to do it you need practice!

## VOLLEYING

One of the most important considerations is the position of the non-striking foot. At the moment of impact you will be standing on one foot only and the power you can get into the shot will depend on how well you have positioned yourself. Once you are set, there is no way you can change the position of your non-hitting leg without losing some impact. This skill can come only with practice. A wall is a help, as you can throw the ball against it and practice volleying the ball back again. Soon you will find you instinctively take up the right position.

Concentrate first on accuracy. There is no point in blazing the ball high, wide and handsome. When you can meet the ball and place it accurately on the volley, then you can

think about power-volleying.

To get the most power into the volley shot, you need to keep your toes pointing downwards and bring the upper part of your foot into contact with the moving ball. The follow-through is not a long one, but you must not snatch at the ball—the volley must be executed smoothly, however quickly you have to move.

Many shots on the volley are taken with the ball coming from the wing, that is, at 90 degrees from the direction you wish to volley it, often at

**1** I have my eye firmly fixed on the ball, attempting to judge the pace of it as it comes towards me in the air and judging where to place my left foot.

waist height. Here you take the ball with your "leading" foot while swivelling toward goal. Accuracy comes with keeping your head as close to the ball as you can—in other words, resist the temptation to lean back—and striking the ball through its center. The usual fault is to strike it low and screw the ball high.

The principle of Bending the Ball can be used and, if the volley is struck accurately in this way, the ball will curve either to the left or right, depending on whether you have used the outside or inside of the foot.

**3** I have swivelled my right hip around and, having kicked the ball, have followed through with the right leg.

**2** Meeting the ball a couple of feet off the ground, I lean back away from the ball and prepare to kick it with the top of my foot.

## Gordon's GEMS

● Timing is all-important in this move, so compose yourself as the ball flies through the air towards you.

● Do not take a wild swipe at the ball. Try "pushing" it through rather than stabbing at it.

● The ideal way to practice this move is to use a wall or have a friend throw the ball to you from a short distance.

# ADVANCED
# SHOOTING SKILLS 2

## THE HALF-VOLLEY

The half-volley is when you kick the ball a split second after it bounces. Like the volley, the half-volley can be used with power and is great to watch when executed successfully.

Making the half-volley is a relatively straightforward skill but a mistimed attempt can make the ball fly off in the wrong direction, so you must judge the flight of the ball correctly and time the kick perfectly.

Watch carefully the flight of the ball and estimate where it will bounce. Sometimes you have the choice of volleying or half-volleying. At other times the bounce will be too far away for you to reach the ball before it bounces, so the half-volley is a necessity.

Your non-kicking foot must be placed close to where the ball bounces; otherwise you will be stretching and off-balance. Bring your kicking leg through to meet the ball an inch or two after the bounce. Because the ball is actually rising as you hit it, the most common fault is skying the ball. Therefore you must get your head right over the ball. The third main requirement is to keep the toe pointing down. Keep your eye on the ball and follow through and you should make a satisfying shot.

Confidence is necessary to play the half-volley and confidence can come only with practice. The first things to acquire are control and accuracy. Our old friend the wall is a great help with practice. Throw or kick the ball against the wall and half-volley it as it comes back to you. Once you have learned to judge the ball correctly you can gradually add power to your kicking.

The half-volley can also be played softly as a pass, and the inside of the foot can be used as an alternative. This move can be practiced conveniently by three players standing in a triangle, passing to each other on the half-volley.

The half-volley is also increasingly used by goalkeepers clearing from hand. With the half-volley, or drop-kick, as compared to the usual punt, the ball is more easily kept low.

**1** The ball is about to bounce in front of me, but just a little too far away for me to hit it on the volley.

**3** My right foot swings through with my foot pointing downward and forward to keep the ball low. Notice I have my head firmly in position even though the ball has gone out of the photograph.

**2** As the ball hits the ground, I have planted my left foot alongside it and I swing my kicking foot through, using the instep to make contact immediately after the ball has struck the ground.

## Gordon's
## GEMS

● Do not allow the ball to hit too far in front of you.

● You can get "swerve" on the half-volley shot if you use the outside of the foot, following the instructions given in the earlier section on Bending the Ball.

● Never lean back when attempting the half-volley.

# CROSSING THE BALL

I would estimate about 80 percent of goals scored in soccer originate from crosses, so obviously this is a very important and productive part of the game. But there is more to crossing a ball than merely getting down the flank and whacking it into the middle in the hope that one of the forwards will be able to get to it.

It is no good crossing the ball when there is no one in the middle to receive it. That would be a waste of your own time and energy and, equally important, you would merely be giving possession of the ball to the opposition.

In situations like this, you need to be brave enough and to have sufficient confidence in your own ability to delay your move in the hope that a teammate will get into a forward position. If nobody is supporting you in the center, then you must quickly decide on a different tactic, possibly cutting in with the ball to shoot yourself, or even winning a corner off a defender.

## END LINE CROSS

The cross that is played in quickly from the end line causes the most confusion to defenders. Because they are running back they will be facing their own goal and unable to organize themselves or mark the strikers properly. As the strikers will be running in towards the ball, they have all the advantages. Making the cross quickly—as opposed to checking back onto your other foot and then crossing—is the more dangerous.

The technique of crossing is important, of course, but the first thing to decide is where to put the ball. The high cross to the far post has been by far the most popular cross. The idea is to clear the goalkeeper for a powerful center-forward to put the ball in. However, the near-post cross for an onrushing striker to head powerfully, or for a striker to glance in or even

**1** I have run with the ball to the perfect position for crossing it into the middle.

**2** The ball has cleared the first defender, which is most important.

head on further across goal is possibly even more productive.

When making the cross, you should get your body facing the direction in which you will kick the ball. For instance, if you are cutting inside parallel with the end line, then you are kicking in the same direction you are running, and the cross is straightforward.

However, often you will be forced to cross at anything up to right angles to the direction of your run. The ball is traveling away from you, so the position of your non-kicking foot is vital. Balance is all-important, as the non-kicking foot must be close to the ball, but at the same time leave room to swing the kicking foot.

If you are crossing from the right, the left foot should be behind and just inside the ball. With your arms spread to maintain balance, and your eyes on the ball, bring your right foot down and across the ball, getting the inside of your foot

under the ball to lift it across the goal. Keep the head down until the move is completed.

Always cross hard—at the worst you could cause the confusion that results in lucky rebounds.

## Gordon's GEMS

● You need good pace on the ball when making the cross into the middle.

● Always try to "swerve" the ball away from the goalkeeper, making it difficult for him to collect.

**3** I have delivered the ball in such a way that it is just too far out for the goalkeeper to collect.

**4** This is the inch-perfect cross, as the ball curls away from the goalkeeper, to be met by the onrushing forward—and it's a goal!

# HEADING THE BALL

**H**eading is vital in soccer, but it is a skill which young players are often not too anxious to learn. Perhaps they think it is not as glamorous as shooting hard or dribbling, but I have a feeling many youngsters fear that heading can be painful, particularly if they do not connect with the ball properly. The first thing to say is that you might do well to practice at first with a light plastic ball. Once you are confident in your technique you will be able to transfer to a proper soccer ball knowing that you can head the ball competently and it will not hurt you.

The point of contact is the forehead—in other words that front part of your head between your eyebrows and your hairline. The skull here is much tougher than the ball, which will give an inch or two on impact, and you will find that you can soon make good headers without the ball hurting at all. Of course, to get the ball in the right place you must keep your eyes open! If you shut your eyes and hope, the ball will strike you rather than the other way around, and if it catches you in an awkward place it could give you a headache.

The neck muscles also come into play when heading. You will have heard of players "attacking" the ball and this is what you must do when heading. You must tense your neck muscles so that they are locked and supporting your head, and strike the ball positively, sending it in the direction you wish with conviction.

Heading the ball is less natural than kicking, and practice makes perfect. Throwing the ball against a wall so that it rebounds just above your head is a good way of practicing alone. You can jump to head the ball back, remembering to thrust your head forward with a positive movement of the neck to get power behind the header. With a friend you can practice heading to each other, or with two friends you can play

**1** About to head the ball, I am leaning backwards in anticipation of using my neck muscles to thrust my head forward to meet the ball.

"piggy in the middle."

Although heading is usually associated with either heading crosses into the net or heading powerfully upfield from defense, do not forget other uses like the headed pass. The ball is often in the air during a game, and can come at you from any angle in any part of the field. If you are marked, without the time to bring the ball under control, you can head a pass to a teammate.

If the ball is just below head height you can stoop. Practice these delicate flicked headers to teammates. Never jump into a header unless you have to—more power and accuracy can be summoned with your feet on the ground.

**2** Hanging in the air, with one leg slightly in front of the other, I have brought my head and the upper part of my body forward to get power into my header, and away the ball goes.

# *Gordon's* GEMS

● Use your forehead to head the ball. You can get more power this way and be more accurate.

● Heading the ball does not hurt, so keep your eyes on the ball.

● Extend your arms to help give you balance when you are in the air.

● Make sure you judge the flight of the ball correctly.

# TACKLING AND
# WINNING THE BALL

**M**any people take tackling for granted but it really is an art in itself and something that you need to give plenty of attention to, and especially so if you are a defender. Remember that the real object of tackling is not just to go in at an opponent but to come away with the ball after the tackle. Timing and technique are as important as strength. It is not always the strongest who emerges with the ball.

But it is essential to go firmly into the tackle. On those unfortunate occasions when a player suffers injury in a tackle it is usually the player who, for some reason, holds back.

**1** Both myself and my opponent have an equal chance of getting the ball—it is what we call a 50-50 situation.

**1** Here I am tracking an opponent who is in possession and running with the ball.

**2** I am now close enough to my opponent and ready to slide in to the tackle and, I hope, win the ball.

**3** Here I go, sliding in with my right foot going past the ball so that I can drag the ball back and win possession.

# THE BLOCK TACKLE

More often than not I harass and annoy opponents rather than use the block tackle and that is mainly because of my size. It would not be much use for me to attempt the block tackle on an opponent who was maybe forty pounds heavier than I am. I would more than likely lose out in the tackle.

The block tackle is used when two players go for the ball and arrive together, both putting their feet to the ball at the same time. When making the block tackle you should try to get your body weight over the top of the ball to add strength to your challenge.

**2** We arrive at the ball at the same time. My foot is at one side of the ball and my opponent has one foot at the other side of it.

**3** The stronger man wins and takes the ball away, having won possession for his team.

**4** I've won the ball and I am about to get to my feet quickly and move away from my opponent, who cannot recover so quickly.

# THE SLIDE TACKLE

There is more to this maneuver than just sliding into an opponent. When you slide in, try to make sure you get your foot around the ball and then get to your feet as quickly as possible to be ready to move away with it.

Key elements in this tackle are surprise and determination, but timing is all important as well. Usually you are coming in from the side or behind as you make this tackle and if your timing is not right you are likely to give away a free kick and that can spell danger for your team.

Sometimes tackles are not about winning the ball, but about stopping an opponent in a dangerous position—for example, an opponent bearing down on goal. It is, of course, doubly important to play the ball in these circumstances, or the penalty for a foul could be disastrous.

# CLOSING DOWN YOUR OPPONENT

**H**ard work is the key to the success of this maneuver. Closing down and pressuring opponents is not the most glamorous part of the game but it is a necessary part and calls for a great deal of hard work by every member of the team. Basically, closing down the opposition means giving the man with the ball as little time and space as possible to play it, and defending his teammates so closely that he has no easy option for a pass. Sooner or later the player on the ball will become frustrated and take a risk—and your team gets a chance to gain possession.

Basically, the strategy stops the opposition from playing and allows you greater opportunity to display your attacking skills, but it will not work effectively if one or two members of your team suddenly feel they are tired and ease off. It takes a united effort from the team as a whole to make it successful and, if done properly, it can be very effective. What you have to do is make sure you mark the opponent closest to you but the plan as a whole is helped if players shout instructions and encouragement to each other—it is very much a team effort.

There are two main systems of defense, called zonal and man-for-man. In the former, each defender patrols one area of the pitch and picks up any attacker who moves into his zone. When the opponent moves into the next zone he is "passed on" to the appropriate defender. If three or four attackers mass into one area, it is impossible for one defender to mark them all. So in practice defenders move into other zones when needed. Often the zonal is combined with some specific man-to-man marking, for example one center back might take the main

responsibility for the opposition's star striker. The system works best with an established defense whose players know each other's styles and habits.

In a man-to-man system each defender marks a specific attacker and follows him everywhere, from one wing to the other if necessary.

Whichever system is in use, forwards and midfielders must be alive to attacks by the opposition midfield or even defenders and be prepared to take on a man and tackle him. None of the opponents must be given time or space to play the ball in comfort.

## Gordon's GEMS

● Don't worry about hard work. If you do plenty of it, it will become a habit and you won't feel it.

● Shout encouragement to teammates, especially if they show signs of tiredness.

● Remember, the quicker you win back the ball, the quicker you can score a goal.

● Try to stay on your feet at all times to keep up the pressure on an opponent.

**1** I notice the player in possession is looking to pass to his teammate on the wing.

**2** By moving in to challenge, I have successfully cut off the ground pass to his teammate.

**3** Having stopped the move, I run in to close my opponent down and try to win possession.

Ten years ago the aim of the throw-in was to try to keep possession. But today the throw-in can also lead directly to a goal, so it has become a very important part of the game in an attacking sense. There are three different types of throw-in—the long, the short and the quick.

The short throw and the quick throw are basically intended to get the ball back in play on the ground and then to keep possession and go on to create a goal-scoring opportunity.

The long throw is used, in the main, anywhere within 30 yards of the goal line in the attacking area. If your team is fortunate enough to have a player who can make a long throw into the penalty area, then the throw-in becomes almost as effective as a corner. If you are too far out to be able to throw the ball into the mouth of the goal, a quick throw to a teammate who can play the ball right away into the center can be used. In either case, a dangerous cross results from the throw.

I would say to any young player, however, that playing for position for a long throw-in is not the way to go about playing soccer. But as a weapon, the long throw-in is a valuable one. Obviously you need someone on your team who is big and strong. I cannot see anyone at the under-10 level managing to throw the ball to the front post, so for younger soccer players, and smaller players like myself, the short and quick throws are the ones for us.

The important thing to remember about having a throw-in is that your side is in possession of the ball. The first priority is to keep it. So do not be hasty. Keep hold of the ball until you can throw it safely to a teammate.

**1** The throw is about to be taken and I move to my left, taking my marker with me.

**2** I have switched directions and am about to lose my marker.

# LOSING YOUR MARKER

Never stand rooted to the spot when waiting for a teammate to make a throw-in because you will give your marker a much better chance of closing in to take up possession.

Movement is the key to throwing off the unwanted attentions of an opponent. As the throw-in is about to be taken, move as though you are going to run in one direction and then switch quickly to go in another.

By doing this you will have a chance of catching your opponent on the wrong foot and taking up possession from the throw-in.

**3** My teammate begins a diversionary run as the ball is thrown towards me.

**4** Here I am free of all opposition and about to take up possession from the throw-in.

## THROWING IN CORRECTLY

It is very easy to lose concentration at a throw-in. It is surprising how many players see the throw-in merely as a routine method of getting the ball back in play, in spite of the possibility of a goal resulting from the throw.

At the least, a throw-in awarded to your team should be a way to ensure that your team keeps possession. And when you consider that any team can expect to take between 20 and 50 throw-ins in a game, you can see the importance of taking care and executing the throw well.

The worst thing you can do when taking a throw-in is to lose possession. And if you forget the basics and lose your concentration, you stand a good chance of making a mess of things and handing the advantage to your opponents.

So the first thing to remember is to concentrate. When making the throw, keep both feet firmly on the ground and behind the touchline as you lift your arms above your head. It may sound unnecessary for me to be explaining this, but even professional players still manage to make a foul throw. They are guilty of handing the ball to their opponents, which is a stupid thing to do.

So when you take a throw, concentrate first on getting the mechanics right. And do not just throw the ball in the general direction of a teammate.

**1** I'm making a quick throw-in but my attacking partner is flat-footed, which shows he is not mentally sharp. We are both at fault—particularly me for throwing the ball at that time.

**2** The ball has landed a couple of feet in front of my teammate, which makes it difficult for him to control it quickly.

Try to make the ball reach him without bouncing. It is much easier for him to control the ball if it comes straight to his head or his foot. If it bounces a yard or so in front of him it is not as easy for him to bring the ball under control quickly and a defender is therefore allowed a little more time to intercept the ball or tackle him.

Do not throw the ball to the side of a teammate on which a defender is guarding him closely. It gives the defender a chance to stretch around and steal the ball.

You cut down the risk of your team's losing possession if the player receiving the ball is in a position to play it back to you right away. If your teammate can do that, then you have made a good throw-in.

● It is not necessary to throw the ball as far as you can. A short throw-in can be just as effective.

● Think of a throw as making a pass with your hands—there is no real excuse for not being accurate.

● As you pick up the ball, look around to see if you can catch the opposition off guard with a quickly taken throw.

**3** The ball bounces into his midriff and he is going to need more touches than he might like before he can get the ball under control.

**4** He now has to play the ball with his left foot and, as that is the side the defender is on, there is more chance of his losing possession.

# TAKING PENALTIES 1

**P**enalty taking is all about being confident and, if you do not feel happy about taking one, then the short answer to that is—don't try it!

Games can be won and lost on penalty kicks so you should be in the right frame of mind—positive and confident—when taking one.

## A SHORT RUN-UP

This is a spot kick I have used on rare occasions and when it succeeds it is great—but you can look very foolish if it fails.

You must have the confidence to attempt this move quickly as the idea is to catch the goalkeeper off his guard.

The short run-up began in Italy, where goalkeepers were getting away with moving early and coming off their line. With the quickly taken penalty, the goalkeeper has less chance of moving. He may even be caught unprepared as you place the ball down, take a couple of paces back and fire the ball into the net. But you must hit the ball with sufficient pace and aim for one of the corners.

## "PLACED" PENALTY

Over the years I have managed to be quite successful at taking penalties and the placed shot is the one I prefer. It has brought me the majority of my spot kick successes and from a general point of view I think this is the most popular and widely used method of trying to score from the penalty spot.

**1** Only after I have relaxed for a moment to concentrate on building up my confidence do I begin my run towards the ball.

**1** I have taken a couple of steps backwards and I'm about to step forward quickly to take aim.

**2** Making contact with the ball, I have aimed for the pole inside the left-hand corner of the goal.

When attempting the placed penalty it is essential that you are confident and positive. I also find you have greater control and accuracy if you use the inside of the foot.

The goalkeeper will do his best to put you off, but concentrate on what you are going to do and, just before you run to the ball, glance at the corner of the goal in which you are not planning to put the ball—with a bit of luck the goalkeeper may decide to dive that way, as you place the ball into the opposite corner.

Another way of deceiving him is to make it look as though you are aiming, say, for the right-hand corner and then to drop your shoulders and place the ball into the opposite corner.

Whatever your preferred method of taking penalties, there are some commonsense things to bear in mind. One is to watch the ball and not the goalkeeper. Lifting your head too soon to see if the ball has gone in is another recipe for a miss.

Do not change your mind about your intentions as you run up. Decide what you want to do and stick to it. Remember that trying to deceive the goalkeeper is fine, but if it affects your rhythm or control it will be counter-productive.

The easiest save for a goalkeeper is around waist height; the hardest is the low shot he has to get down to. Aim for the stanchion at the back of the net. If in doubt which side to put the ball, assume the goalkeeper is right-handed and therefore happier diving to his right.

**2** I make it look as though I am going to aim the ball just inside the goalkeeper's left-hand post, making him tense himself to dive that way.

**3** At the last second I change direction and with the inside of the foot kick the ball to the goalkeeper's right, sending him the wrong way.

**3** The ball is on its way into the left-hand corner of the net and the goalkeeper has been caught by surprise.

**4** The goalkeeper has hardly moved and can only watch as the ball hits the back of the net. Another penalty success!

# *TAKING PENALTIES 2*

## THE BLASTED PENALTY

The penalty kick that is blasted towards goal is one I do not particularly care for. I feel the penalty taker loses some accuracy when concentrating solely on power and this allows the goalkeeper a better chance.

However, this type of penalty does produce the goods provided it is executed correctly. The secret of success with the fiercely struck penalty kick is to make up your mind where you are going to put the ball and then keep your eyes on the ball when you take the kick. Do not look at the goalkeeper and remember to follow through with the kicking leg.

All the spectators, if any, plus the other players, will be watching closely when you take a penalty. Shut them all out of your mind and concentrate solely on the task of scoring.

Confidence is of the essence with a spot kick and confidence comes with practice. Practicing penalties is quite easy, particularly if you have a goalkeeping friend who wants to practice stopping them!

## THE GOALKEEPER'S VIEW

How does the goalkeeper set about saving a penalty? From his point of view, luck plays an important part—he has no prospect of saving a perfectly struck penalty, so he must hope, first, that the kicker gives him a chance.

Most goalkeepers have a preferred method they will use most of the time. The most popular

**1** Having made up my mind what part of the goal I am going to put the ball into I make my run towards the ball.

**2** Contact has been made with the ball and I have put everything into the shot to give the ball plenty of pace.

is to commit in advance to diving one way. The theory is that if they guess right they will have their bodyweight on the correct leg and stand a chance of making a save.

Other goalkeepers prefer to react to the kick, confident that their reflexes will give them a chance of reaching anything that is not hit too hard. Some stand their ground for another reason. They figure that it is almost impossible to save a shot near the corner, but they can reach anything, however well struck, if it is close enough to them. And it is true that many successful penalties are scored with straight shots which go in because the goalkeeper has dived to one side.

The last clue a goalkeeper has comes from watching the kicker's foot as it comes to the ball—with experience he will know from the angle of the foot the likely trajectory of the ball. Finally, when he dives, he should dive slightly forward, not along the goal line—if he touches the ball with his fingers he will have a better chance of deflecting it wide rather than into the net.

## Gordon's GEMS

● Decide where you are going to hit the ball and don't let anything put you off. Go for it.

● Do not change your mind when you are running up to kick the ball.

● Keep your eye on the ball and make sure you are well over the ball when you make contact.

**3** I have made sure that my kicking leg has followed through. This is essential if you are to give the ball pace.

**4** The goalkeeper has chosen the correct side to dive but because of the pace of the ball he is beaten and it is a goal.

## CURLING AROUND THE WALL

I explained earlier in the book how to "bend" or "curl" the ball. If you studied that section and worked on the movement you will be able to curl free kicks around a defensive wall in games.

Mastering the art of bending a ball takes a lot of practice, and when you are young you will not find this skill quite so easy to acquire as the player will who is older and stronger.

Nevertheless, if you can develop this ability at an early age it will stand you in good stead later when there will be more opportunity to put it to use in games.

Combining power with curl is difficult, because you are making contact with the outside of the ball, rather than striking firmly through the center. Power comes from increasing the speed of the foot, from following through forcefully, and from the angle of the foot. The more upright the foot as it kicks the ball, the more power can go into the kick.

If you put the time in working at this move, and have determination and confidence, there is no reason why you should not become proficient at it. Off the field, you can practice the skill by using a trash can or some other obstacle as the "wall." When you come to use it in a game, my advice is to aim the ball a couple of feet outside the goal post and, if you have kicked the ball as it should be kicked, the "curl" will bring it back on target for goal.

Every free kick near the penalty area is not an invitation to try to score directly. Sometimes a surprise chip to a teammate will pay dividends.

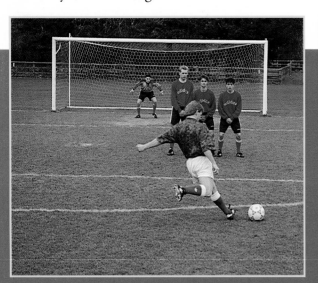

**1** Having picked my spot, I am about to strike the ball with the inside of my foot.

**2** The ball is played a couple of feet outside the post and I follow through with my kicking leg.

# DEFENDING WITH A WALL

The idea of a defensive wall was forced on soccer when players developed the technique of shooting with great power from 25 yards or so. The wall is intended to block as much of the goal as possible and reduce the target for the kicker.

The wall is not a haphazard line of as many players as happen to be nearby, but a carefully thought-out defense worked on in practice, so that all members of the team will know where to form the wall for a free kick in any particular place. It is a good plan to have a player responsible for the wall, to work in co-operation with the goalkeeper, who will decide how many players are needed. The wall is usually built to cover the near side of the goal, while the goalkeeper guards the far side. It is best formed of attackers and midfielders, leaving the skilled defenders free to cover the opponents not involved in taking the kick. The number of players in the wall is a vital decision. Some free kickers are so expert that as many as six players might be required to line up, leaving only four defenders free to look after as many as six or seven opponents.

Each man in the wall must know his role, too, and be disciplined in carrying it out. One or two will charge at the kicker to try to knock the ball down—but they must be careful not to charge before the kick.

Others must keep their places. Those at the end of the line, for example, must not peel off too early and leave a gap. On the other hand, they must be ready to spring into attack once the ball is safely cleared.

**3** The ball has now "curled" back and is going into the net just underneath the bar.

## Gordon's GEMS

● Aim two feet wide of the post. The "curl" you expect to get on the ball will bring it back on course.

● Try not to hit the "wall" with your shot — It is a waste of a good scoring chance.

● Make sure you follow through with your kicking leg after making the shot.

# TAKING FREE KICKS 2

## ADDING MEN TO THE WALL

Adding attackers to a defensive wall can be a successful ploy. Lining up one or two men on the end of the wall works well, especially if you have someone who can hit the ball hard and accurately. The goalkeeper does not see the ball until late and often there is no time for him to make a save.

Sometimes the attacker closest to the wall can push against the wall while the player on the outside edge of the wall peels away just as the penalty is taken. This leaves a gap for the ball to go through, but be careful not to be drawn into a shoving match with the defenders. Your team has a chance to score—don't waste it.

The attacking team has a big advantage at free kicks, because they have several players free while the defending team has to tie up so many in the wall. Other methods to beat the wall include the chipped shot to the corner farthest from the goalkeeper, or the chip over the wall to a team-mate running around the wall to head the ball at goal. Moves involving teammates should be carefully worked out and rehearsed in training.

The illustration opposite shows a free kick move I was involved in which scored in an important match. It is a good example of a move which can be practiced and used. Player 1 feints to take the kick but runs over the ball. Player 2 takes the kick—a pass to Player 3, who immediately passes to Player 1, who has continued his run. He crosses to Player 4, who has run in toward goal and who scores.

**1** The defenders are lined up to protect the right half of the goal and we add two attackers to the left side of the wall to hinder the goalkeeper's view.

**2** A gap is created as one attacker peels away and the other pushes into the defenders in the wall.

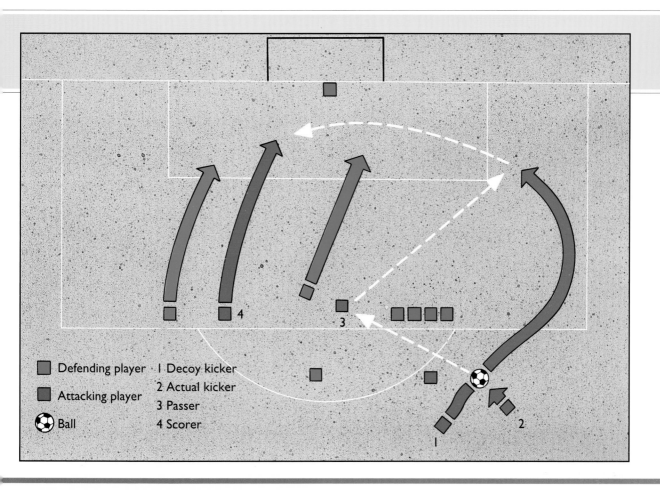

Defending player
Attacking player
⚽ Ball

1 Decoy kicker
2 Actual kicker
3 Passer
4 Scorer

**3** The ball is through and on its way to the goal, leaving the goalkeeper with a hard task.

# *Gordon's* GEMS

● If you are an attacker on the end of a wall you should remember to be alert at all times.

● Wait as long as you can before peeling away, so that the ball is kept from the goalkeeper's view as long as possible.

● If you are taking the free kick, put plenty of pace on the ball—and be accurate.

# TAKING CORNERS 1

Corner kicks are an important and very productive part of any team's armory. Near post corners, back post corners, short corners—get the best out of them. Being on the short side and therefore not able to get many penalty-area headers in, I have often had to take corners.

Accuracy is of paramount importance if you are to make the most of corner kicks. The kicker has to be able to pick out teammates either at the near post or the back post; otherwise the defending team have a much easier chance of clearing the danger.

It is important, of course, that you and your teammates know which type of corner you are about to take.

## THE NEAR POST CORNER

I find the near post corner is a particularly dangerous one. It is difficult to defend against if you have the right players to execute the move.

If you station a couple of big men at the near post and aim the ball to them, it is very difficult for the goalkeeper to come and collect the ball. These men should be strong and have good control with their heads. The idea is to hit one of your own men at the near post and for him to flick the ball on with his head.

**1** I have taken the corner kick and the ball is on its way towards the near post.

**2** My two teammates waiting at the near post watch closely as the ball drops towards them.

That is the first part of the operation. Once you have got a successful flick on at the near post, you need a player who is fearless and athletic flying in at the back post. You need someone who sees nothing but the ball and goes for it without thinking about his personal safety.

Practicing near post corner kicks can be boring but, when you pull one off in a game and it leads to a goal, you get a tremendous feeling of satisfaction. Taking advantage of your set plays goes a long way towards winning games.

The near post corner is hard to defend against. A defender must be at the near post to deal with curling inswingers and the hard low drive—he is most effective not holding the post but slightly infield. Another defender should be near the edge of the six-yard box to guard against the flick-on. His big problem is whether to stay goalside of the man he is marking, thus conceding the attacker the chance to make first contact, or move in front of his man.

## *Gordon's* GEMS

● Accuracy from the corner is of paramount importance if the kick is to have a chance of succeeding. You must be able to pick out the near post attacker every time with your kick.

● Don't waste a good attacking opportunity by overhitting the kick. That would give the goalkeeper a better chance of collecting the ball.

● If you are the player arriving to head the ball towards the goal, make sure you are not put off by defenders.

**3** One of my teammates, who is blocking the path of the goalkeeper, gets the first flick-on with his head.

**4** Seeing the ball flicked on, another attacker comes in at the back post to head the ball. (On this occasion, however, it has gone over the bar!)

# TAKING CORNERS 2

## FAR POST CORNER

This is the basic corner kick and is used when you believe that your best header of the ball can beat the opposing team's best header of the ball.

It is important to have players at the front post, in order to keep the defense guessing and to block the goalkeeper's view and make it more difficult for him to come off his line and intercept the ball.

Movement before the kick is very important if you are the striker. It gives the taker of the kick a signal of your intention and helps him aim the kick towards you. It also helps you to lose your marker. Always be on your toes to avoid your marker's getting too close to you.

It is not too often that goals are scored at the far post by headers direct from the corner kick, but there is always the chance of a knock-down to cause havoc in the defense so that other players might be able to swipe a goal.

Curl can be put on the ball, so that it curls in toward goal or curls away, perhaps tempting the goalkeeper to come out to intercept a ball that he then finds he cannot reach.

Do not place the ball too near the goalkeeper, who has the obvious advantage of being able to use his hands. Mix up your corners to keep the defense guessing.

## THE QUICKLY TAKEN CORNER

**1** My team have won a corner and, as I make my way to the corner, I look around to see whether I can take the kick quickly.

**2** A teammate is alert to my thinking and I immediately aim the ball towards him.

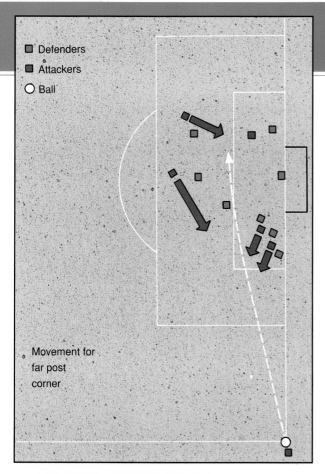

Defenders
Attackers
○ Ball

Movement for
far post
corner

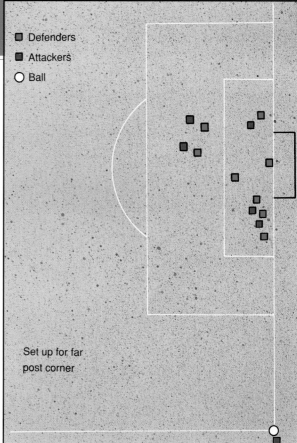

Defenders
Attackers
○ Ball

Set up for far
post corner

**3** He has come towards me to meet the ball and quickly plays it back to me.

**4** In turn, I hit the ball low into the six-yard area where another teammate is waiting.

# PLAYING IN DEFENSE

**M**any coaches will tell you that if you are building a successful team you begin first of all with the defense. I am not about to argue with that belief.

Defense is a very important part of any team. The main job of a central defender is to prevent goals. This might sound obvious, but what I want to emphasize is the secondary nature of everything else. A tall central defender who scores occasionally from set plays is valuable, but he is no good if he also concedes goals.

Lee Chapman struggles to make an impression against Steve Bould and David Hillier, who are marking him closely.

If you play central defender, remember the simple thing is always best. Get the ball away, even if you concede a corner or throw-in. Do not overelaborate or be too ambitious. Doing the unexpected might bamboozle the opposition but it might also confuse your teammates, and confusion is the last thing you want in your own penalty area.

Fullbacks must also give priority to their defensive duties, which include covering for the central defenders. But a fullback often has a particular opponent to mark—the opposition's wide striker on his side of the field. He must make sure his opponent gets as little of the ball as possible, so the fullback must be able to read the game accurately.

A fullback is also expected to become a wide attacker at times. He is often the man who can bypass the midfield and get deep into opposition territory and make telling centers. So if you play fullback you must be mobile, fast and able to cross the ball.

All the defenders must be able to tackle, so practice this skill. But a tackler must also learn discretion. The worst thing you can do is to commit yourself to the tackle and be beaten, thus giving your teammates an extra man to contend with while you are out of play.

Defending is a team operation, so the best you can do for your teammates is to keep between the goal and your opponent, denying him a clear run at goal. When he is in possession, try to jockey him into positions where he cannot be dangerous. Restrict his space.

To be a successful defender you must develop a good understanding with your fellow defenders. The more you play together the better the understanding should become. Knowing what your fellow defenders are capable of, what they are likely to do, and where they will be is

One of the greatest defenders in world soccer is Paolo Maldini of Milan. Pace, anticipation and determination make him an outstanding opponent.

the key to this success. Another important ingredient is communication. Players who shout instructions on the field are a great help.

Try to size up the situation when you haven't got the ball and if you think you can assist a teammate by shouting an instruction to him then do so. It might be a case of warning him of a likely challenge, or it may be to tell him to pass the ball to a certain player.

When the high ball is coming at you and you feel you are in a better position to deal with it than a fellow defender, shout and let him know that. You will then avoid having two men going for the same ball.

Most teams will develop a defense which relies mainly on either marking opposing players or space. Sometimes it is necessary to do both, searching for a position that allows you to get tight on your opponent if he gets the ball, but at the same time allows you to provide cover for colleagues. The art of marking is to position yourself most effectively to prevent your opponent's threatening the goal, so mostly you will be goalside of him to intercept any runs he might make.

Always try to remain part of a compact unit as a defender, and not detached so that the defense is stretched. This is of greatest importance if the defensive play is to move up and close down the opposition in their own half and deny their forwards room. This means the opposing strikers always have to be worried about being caught offside, but it also means the defenders have to work smoothly as a unit. One defender hanging back a couple of yards can put a forward on the opposite side of the field onside and free for an unchallenged run on goal.

Soccer is a team game and you will be a better player if you remember that.

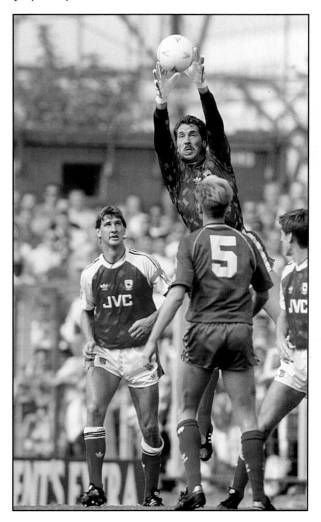

Two reasons why Arsenal have an outstanding defense—David Seaman, the goalkeeper, and central defender Tony Adams.

# GORDON'S BEST TEAM

Since I made my debut for Dundee in 1972, I have been lucky enough to play for leading clubs in Scotland and England, and because of these clubs' successes in European competition I have played against some of the best club sides in the world.

Add my 50 international matches for Scotland and appearances in two World Cup finals tournaments, and you will appreciate that I have played against most of the world's outstanding players of the last 15 years or so. My great regret is that Pele retired before I could share a field with him.

On these pages I have selected my best team from the players I opposed in those years.

In goal I would have big Pat Jennings, whose astonishing career lasted 25 years. He finally retired in 1986 after a World Cup finals clash with Brazil, the last of his 119 international matches for Northern Ireland. His agility and size, which included hands big enough to pluck the ball out of the air one-handed, plus his dependability and amiable temperament, made him a very special player.

My back four would include Manuel Amoros on the right. He was an outstanding player in the French teams of the 1980s, which were good enough to win the World Cup, but didn't quite last the distance. Amoros, in addition to his defensive abilities, was a very fast and powerful raider, with a strong shot.

On the left I would have Paolo Maldini, who is still piling up honors with Milan, his only club, and Italy. He followed in his father's footsteps in winning a European Cup medal with Milan. A highly polished player, he, too, has the ability to move from defense to attack.

His Milan colleague, and another one-club man, Franco Baresi, would be one of my center backs, a veteran sweeper whom the Italians are reluctant to allow to retire, so well does he

Kenny Dalglish was the best I ever played with or against in British football.

organize his club's and country's defenses.

His partner would be another unflappable player, Alan Hansen, one of the smoothest players you could wish to see, a man who combined safe defense with a flair for carrying the ball forward in surprise attacks.

In midfield, there has been none better than Michel Platini, a player with all the skills, and rightly voted, three times running, European Footballer of the Year in the 1980s. I think Platini was the main inspiration of the revival in the French national team's fortunes during this time.

Partnering him would be Bryan Robson, a man whose whole-hearted commitment was never blunted by some unlucky injuries. He scored many vital goals, including the quickest ever in a World Cup finals match, when he scored after only 27 seconds for England against France.

Up front I would play Chris Waddle of

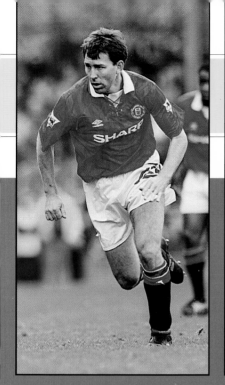

Bryan Robson's strength and courage were an inspiration in my Manchester United days.

It would be difficult to think of a more difficult marking job than Diego Maradona. Remember his second goal against England in the '86 World Cup?

Taking on Franco Baresi would be most forwards' worst nightmare!

## GORDON'S BEST XI

### GOALKEEPER
Pat Jennings (*Northern Ireland*)

### BACK FOUR
Manuel Amoros (*France*)
Franco Baresi (*Italy*)
Alan Hansen (*Scotland*)
Paolo Maldini (*Italy*)

### MIDFIELD
Michel Platini (*France*)
Bryan Robson (*England*)

### FORWARDS
Chris Waddle (*England*)
Marco Van Basten (*Holland*)
Diego Maradona (*Argentina*)
Kenny Dalglish (*Scotland*)

England to exploit the wings. He is another skillful player whose dribbling talents can demoralize defenses.

Kenny Dalglish would be another to provide craft in the front line. He had everything—possibly the best and most consistent player I came across in my few hundred matches in Britain.

Diego Maradona is acknowledged to be the world's outstanding player of the mid-1980s, and nobody who saw his performances for Argentina in the 1986 World Cup can doubt that he is among the game's immortals. He must be in the side.

Finally, all this array of talent would need is a man guaranteed to put the ball in the opposition net at the slightest opportunity. Marco Van Basten has scored some outstanding goals for Milan and Holland in recent years—a player with the skill to match his power, a natural scorer.

# PREPARATION AND ATTITUDE

Having the right kind of preparation for games is, of course, vital for professional soccer players but it is also important for young players.

When you are young you will probably have the right kind of preparation because parents usually insist that their children get to bed early anyway because of school. So you should be in good shape.

Anyone under the age of 14 should not really have much of a problem because of the lifestyle they lead up to that age. As you get older you should begin to prepare yourself, as games will be getting harder, there will be a lot more running involved and it is bound to be much more physical.

## DIET

Remember to treat your body like an engine and put the right fuel in. If you put the wrong stuff in, it will break down. If you put diesel into a gas engine you will not get the best of results! The body's fuel is food.

So take care to look after your body with proper rest and diet before games. Get enough rest and sleep the night before a game and do not eat too much before playing. My diet as a soccer player is, perhaps, well known because it has received a lot of publicity in newspapers in recent years.

I start out in the morning by eating a bowl of hot cereal, made with milk, and with bananas mixed in. Believe it or not, most people who have tried it, like it!

At lunchtime, before a game, I have a bowl of fresh fruit salad, though sometimes, during the coldest of the winter months, I will have a poached egg on toast. On the day before a game I eat pasta but without sauce. Plain pasta with a bit of butter on it is the order of the day for me.

During the week my diet usually consists of cereal and bananas in the morning, a piece of toast at lunchtime, and meat—usually chicken—and pasta at night.

I eat a lot of pasta, which gives me plenty of energy. Putting on weight is not a problem if I am doing a lot of running because I burn off the energy it gives me. In summer, when I am not playing, I stay off the pasta.

Gone are the days, I'm afraid, when players were told to eat steak. When I was a rookie, living in rooms all week, I used to love pregame meals because the pregame meal was probably the best meal of the week and I used to overindulge in the steak, even though it was only about three hours before a game.

You will probably know yourself the sort of foods to avoid. Fatty foods, candies, sweet sugary drinks and numerous snacks are not good things to eat or drink if you wish to preserve your fitness at its highest. And I hope it isn't necessary, by the way, to point out to any youngster the dangers of smoking and alcohol.

## REST

I am lucky in that, as a professional, I can take a nap a couple of afternoons a week. I know it is a bit more difficult for beginners, but if you are a serious player then you should try to get some decent sleep at night. I try to get my best sleep—and usually succeed—on a Thursday night

play well in every game. No one can, no matter who he is.

If you don't play well, then fair enough, but you can still win if you have given 100 percent effort. It is easier to sit down after a game and face your teammates, or your coach, if you know you have given everything you can and tried your hardest.

Years ago I used to get very upset if I did not play well, but an assistant coach told me that the only thing you can guarantee is trying all the time. That is something I have never forgotten.

## FITNESS

I have not mentioned in this section on preparation the need to keep physically fit and to practice. This is because I hope these requirements are obvious.

Nobody can play soccer seriously if he is not fit, and I have emphasized throughout this book the need to

before a Saturday game. I am not against players staying up late the night before a game as long as they are relaxing.

## MENTAL PREPARATION

When kick-off time approaches it is important to be in the right frame of mind for the game—and that means being confident of winning.

One thing you have to remember, however, is that you cannot guarantee to yourself, your coach or your teammates that you are going to

practice. Let me assure you again that I still practice, even after 20 years as a professional player.

In this book, I hope I have sufficiently stressed the importance of playing together as a team. If you start doing things for yourself in a game, then the time has come for you to think again. You must always play for the team, not yourself.

On the other hand, I am a great believer in young players using games to practice and learn in. Concentrate on developing your skills and do not be afraid to experiment.

# INDEX